Football, The Basics for Women

Football, The Basics for Women

S. Green

American Football, The Basics for Women
S. Green

Destiny Publishing, LLC

International Standard Book Number:
ISBN-13: 978-0578086880
ISBN-10: 0578086883

Author: Sarah A. Green
Editor: Jennifer Singleton-jennifersingleton.net
Illustrations: VIP Productions
Cover Art: ©iStockphoto.com/**Artist-Nikola Miljkovic**
POD Company: Create Space

DEDICATION

This book is dedicated to three people who have been
very special in my life. My mother,
Margurite Hutchinson; my brother, Ronald Green;
and my cousin Damitra Santiago.

Thank you for your life-long
support of all my endeavors.

Other Books by this Author

American Football, The Basics

Fútbol Americano, Conocimientos Básicos

Table of Contents

Acknowledgements

**Thanks to God, without Whom,
I can do nothing.**

I extend thanks to everyone, mentioned and unmentioned, who
helped me in the writing of this book.

Special thanks to Joseph Butler, Ronald Green and
Rashad Bolden; football fathers, little league coaches,
and avid football fans for all of their assistance
in helping me understand the game of football.

Thanks to Melissa Hughes for all of her
encouragement and sage advice.

Thanks to my editor Jennifer Singleton
who has been an excellent source
of help and information.

How this Book was Born

This book was conceived in 2009, when the New Orleans Saints, my home team, after over 40 years in existence finally had a winning season which led to a Super Bowl championship win.

That entire football season was a magical time for the city of New Orleans and the entire gulf coast region, which was still recovering from the effects of Hurricane Katrina.

While nearly 5 years had gone by since the hurricane, many people were still rebuilding their homes and their lives. A winning team seemed to be both an escape and an energizer.

Although difficult life issues continued to exist and people had the same problems during the football season that they had before, things didn't seem so bad because the Saints were winning! On the street, in the supermarket, at the coffee shop, people walked around smiling for no reason and they couldn't wait for Sunday to arrive. Magical seems to be the only appropriate word to describe that time.

I was never a big football fan. My favorite sport to watch had always been tennis. I watched the Saints games on Sundays, but always with the remote in my hand so I could flip to the game when it looked like they would score and change the channel when it looked like the other team would score. My understanding of what the players actually did on the field was minimal. The only things I really knew were when to cheer for a touchdown and how to sigh with relief when the game ended with the Saints on top. Other than that, I was at a loss.

After the Saint's Super Bowl win, I became interested in this game. I found it fun to watch, the fans were extremely passionate about it, and we had a team that would probably win several more championships in the coming years. I needed to understand it better.

I studied everything I could about football the entire following summer and watched every game I could throughout the next season. I completely submerged myself in football.

Quickly I realized that many of the books written on the subject, having been written by experts; former players and coaches, were written in a football language that I did not understand. It seemed that they were meant to be read by other football experts and long-time fans of the sport and not by a novice of the game as I was.

I thought, *maybe there are other people like me who don't know anything and need to have this game explained to them from the preschool level.* So I sought other sources. I overwhelmed my brothers and cousins and uncles with questions about the game. I OD'd on NFL radio and TV. I attended football seminars; I recorded games and watched them over and over again, studying carefully, what each player did on the field. The dots began to connect and I began to understand the game.

The learning process was fun and exhilarating; and by the end of this project, I found that I was something I never would have predicted I would be in this life; a football fan. A football fanatic!

Now *I'm* one of those people who can't wait 'til Sunday, not because I'm anxious to go to church, but shamefully, because I can't wait to watch football. I'm a bona fide TV yeller who thinks every call against my team is a wrong one; and while not confident enough to participate in the regular debates the men in my family have about football, I can at least listen to their discussion and not hear, "blah, blah, blah, blah, blah".

While football can be a very complicated sport, I finally get the passion one can develop for it. The comparison I've heard so often of it being like a chess match seems very accurate.

I do not profess to be a master of this sport, but hopefully the information you gain from reading this book, will at least allow you to watch and understand this great sport and perhaps someday enjoy it as much as I do.

Happy reading.

S. Green

Introduction

The old cliché about the way to a man's heart being through his stomach is something moms have passed down for countless generations. And while I'm not in any way out to dispel this saying, I believe that sports can be another way to your guy's heart. In my experience, I have found that having common interests can make a relationship fun and enjoyable in a way that other things, which may be considered more important, cannot. Of course every relationship needs the biggies: love, trust, respect, etc., but having a partner who likes doing some of the same things you like doing not only makes relationships more fun, but *life* more fun.

If you're like me, you're a girl with a guy who loves watching sports.

Though most men have one or two favorites, as long as they can watch a sports game that involves a ball bouncing, rolling, or being projected into the air, they'll think that particular sport is the best thing since sliced bread.

And if you're like me, you're a girl who has a really good guy who notices you Tuesday through Saturday during football season, but on Sundays and Mondays (Monday night football), you have to dress like a football and hold a beer in each hand if you want to get that same attention.

Maybe you're a girl who will never love football, or any other sport for that matter, the same way your guy does; but you still want to be a part of the enjoyment he experiences when he watches it.

Girls, this book is written for you.

This book will have served its purpose if it helps you to at least learn enough about the basics of the sport of football, if that's the sport your guy enjoys, to occasionally watch a game with him, understand what's happening, and discuss the game without asking questions all the way through.
Believe it or not, I was in the same boat as you not too long ago.

Learning about the sport of football has given me a great appreciation for the game and its players. I understand now how it can be so addictive to its fans. I watch football all the time now and it's really lots of fun having something new to share with my guy.

I wish you good luck in love and best wishes for more mutual football enjoyment in your relationship.

1

History:
What is Football?

Football is a sport enjoyed in many countries around the world. However, its largest following is in the United States. There are professional leagues for the sport both in the United States and Canada. The National Football League, or NFL, is the largest of the professional football leagues in the U.S. and was formed in 1966 when two opposing leagues merged to form one.
Its football season begins in August and runs through February.

As football is primarily considered to be an American sport, to help increase its popularity around the globe, the NFL has sponsored various promotional activities including holding both exhibition and regular season games in other countries.
Because of their efforts, football is growing worldwide and gaining new fans every year.

While there are many different sports available to enjoy today, some which may be considered more popular in other parts of the world; football holds a very beloved and passionate place in the hearts of its fans. For this reason, millions of avid fans travel to attend games in person or congregate at home or in sports bars weekly to watch and/or participate in this sport.

Football has its origins in the sport of rugby. Walter Camp, a coach at Yale University in the late 19th century, is known as the father of football. He, along with several generations of other coaches and players of the game formed, through a combination of rule creations and rule changes from the sport of rugby; the sport we now enjoy today called football. Camp was influential in helping to create many of the rules of college football and is credited with creating many rules now universally used in college and professional football in the United States.
Yards gained on downs, the points system, the arrangement of offensive players on the field, and the use of officials are just a few of the parts of the game said to be influenced by him.

Since the early beginnings of the game, the sport of football has been an ever-expanding and ever-evolving sport. The skill, schemes, and planning it takes for teams to be successful at this sport has made it one of the most innovative and consuming of the popular sports games of today. Its constant growth has made it interesting and enjoyable for enthusiasts throughout the world.

2

The NFL

The NFL is composed of 32 teams from cities all over the United States. The teams are divided into 2 conferences, the AFC (American Football Conference) and the NFC (National Football Conference).
The AFC and NFC are further are divided into 4 divisions:

AFC North, AFC South, AFC East, and AFC West
NFC North, NFC South, NFC East, and NFC West

There are 4 teams within each division. These 4 teams play each other 2 times per season, and play other teams outside their division and their conference. The NFL football season consists of 4 preseason games that do not count in terms of the regular season's wins and losses.
(Preseason games are usually used to evaluate potential players to determine whether they will make the team and prepare starting players for the upcoming regular season.)

There are 16 regular season games that do count. Each team receives one week off from play during the season, which is called a "bye" week.

The Super Bowl

Throughout the season, the teams have an opportunity to compete for division titles, conference titles, and the overall championship, the Super Bowl. The competition for titles proceeds as follows:

- The teams with the best overall record for their division win the division title (division championship).
- The winner of each division title wins an opportunity to compete in the post season (playoffs).
- There are 2 "wildcard" or free-entry positions to the playoffs available in each conference (AFC or NFC), for the 2 teams with the best record that did not win their division titles.
- In the playoffs, the remaining top-winning teams of each conference compete against each other to make it to their conference's NFC or AFC championship game.
- The winners of each conference championship game compete against each other in the final championship of the season, the Super Bowl.
- The team that wins the Super Bowl is considered the league and world champions for that football season.

The Lombardi Trophy

The Lombardi Trophy is the coveted prize awarded to the Super Bowl championship team. The trophy is created by Tiffany & Company and depicts a regulation-size football that is made entirely of sterling silver.

The Lombardi Trophy is named after legendary football coach Vince Lombardi who, as head coach of the Green Bay Packers, won the first two Super Bowl Championships in 1967 and 1968. Following his sudden death in 1970, the trophy was renamed in his honor from World Championship Trophy to the Vince Lombardi Trophy. While the trophy is awarded on the field to the winning team after each Super Bowl game, it is returned to Tiffany & Company for a personalized engraving of the team's name and the Super Bowl's date and final score.

The words "Vince Lombardi Trophy" and the NFL shield are engraved at the base of the trophy.

After completion, the trophy is sent back to the winning team for them to keep.

The Pro Bowl

The Pro Bowl is the NFL "All-star" game and is held at the end of the football season. This game is held the week prior to the Super Bowl. Players are selected for participation by a combination of votes from coaches, other players, and fans. The Pro Bowl game pits the season's best players against each other. The players are selected by a draft style selection process in which two retired veteran alums serve as captains of two teams and draft from a pool of players voted in as Pro Bowl players for that football season.

Participating in the Pro Bowl is considered an honor as the players for this game are usually considered to be the best at their positions

3

Game Structure and Players

A regulation football game consists of 22 players, 11 players from each team, made up of one team's offensive players and the other team's defensive players. The basic objective of the offense is to advance the ball down the 100-yard field toward the opposing team's *end zone* to score points. The defense's job is to prevent the other team from gaining yards toward their end zone and/or take the ball away from the other team's offense, move the ball in the opposite direction, and score points for *their* team.

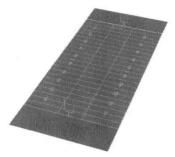

Each football team is divided into 3 separate and distinct units:

- The offense, whose primary duty is to score points for the team
- The defense, whose primary duty is to prevent the opposing team from scoring points
- The special teams unit, whose primary responsibility is to kick the ball in the form of kickoffs, punts and field goals.

The Game/Play Clock

Quarters

The game is divided into 4 quarters or four 15-minute increments of regulation time. The game clock does not run continuously, but stops each time the ball is ruled "dead", or out of play. Each team is allowed 3 time-outs per half.

Halftime

There is a 15-minute break at the end of the second quarter, called halftime. During halftime the two teams have an opportunity to return to the locker room to rest and create a strategy for the second half of the game.

Two Minute Warning

The two minute warning occurs during the final 2 minutes of the first and second half of the game (the end of the 2nd and 4th quarters) and is used as a way of letting the teams know how much time remains on the clock before halftime or the end of the game. During the two minute warning, the game clock is stopped at the two minute mark or immediately following if the ball is in play when the clock reaches the two minute mark. During this time in the game, the coaches are not allowed to challenge questionable plays on the field. Questionable plays must go through a, "booth review" or a review by NFL officials that are not on the field, but those located in the control center or control *booth.*

Player Positions

Offense- The team with possession of the ball

❖ **Quarterback (QB)-**The leader of the team. The quarterback signals at the line of scrimmage and receives the ball from the center. The quarterback hands the ball to the running back, throws it to the receiver, and occasionally runs with it towards the end zone.

❖ **Center (C)-**The player who snaps/hikes the ball to the quarterback and blocks defensive players while the quarterback runs the play.

❖ **Running Back (RB)-**The player who runs with the football to gain yardage downfield.

❖ **Full Back (FB)**-The player who's responsible for blocking for the running back and also for pass-blocking to protect the quarterback.

❖ **Wide Receiver (WR)**-The player who uses his speed and quickness to elude defenders and catch the football.

❖ **Tight end** (TE)-The player who serves as a receiver and a blocker.

❖ **Left guard (LG)/Right guard (RG)**-The inner two members of the offensive line whose jobs are to block for and protect the quarterback and ball carriers.

❖ **Left tackle (LT)/Right tackle (RT)**-The outer two members of the offensive line whose jobs are to block for and protect the quarterback and ball carriers.

Defense- The team without possession of the ball

❖ **Defensive Tackle (DT)-**The inner two members of the defensive line, whose jobs are to stop a running play or attempt to sack the quarterback.

❖ **Defensive End (DE)-**The outer two members of the defensive line whose job is to overcome offensive blocking, stop a running play, or to attempt to sack the quarterback.

❖ **Linebacker (LB)-**These players line up to assist in defending the run and the pass.

❖ **Safety (S)-**The players who line up in the back field and defend the long pass and the run.

❖ **Cornerback (CB)-**The players who line up on the wide parts of the field and defend against the offensive wide receivers.

Defense

Line of Scrimmage

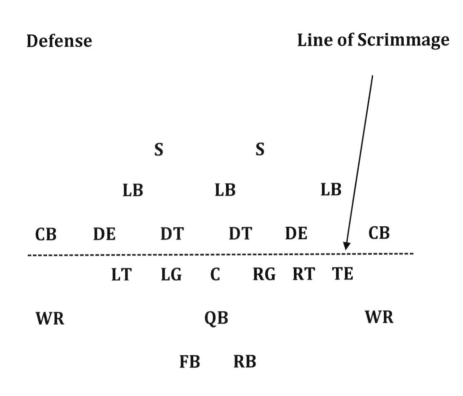

Offense

> The above image depicts a typical player line-up of the offensive and defensive units of a team.

4

How the Game is Played

Kickoff

At the beginning of the game, an official meets leaders of both teams on the field and makes a coin toss. Whichever team wins the coin toss decides on whether their team will:

- Kick the ball to begin play
- Receive the kicked ball to begin play
- Defer their decision to kick or receive until the second half of the game.

The decision to defer is usually made due to a team wanting to leave the kicking or receiving option available for one of two reasons: gaining a perceived wind or weather advantage during the second half by choosing which direction to which the ball will be kicked; or putting the defense on the field first to provide an advantageous field position for the offense based on how the game has gone for their team during the first half.

If the defer option is selected by the team winning the coin toss, the other team decides whether to kick or receive to begin play for the first half of the game.

The defense kicks the ball, the offense receives the ball. Once the ball is kicked, the receiving team (offense) has the following 3 options to begin play:

- If the ball is caught in the field of play, a player may attempt to immediately run the ball down field to try to gain additional yards from the place where the ball was caught.
- If the ball is caught in the field of play, a player may catch the ball and wave his arm to signal a *fair catch*, indicating that he will not attempt to advance the ball, thereby avoiding all tackling attempts. (Play begins from the spot of the fair catch.)
- If the ball is caught in the receiving team's end zone a receiver may opt to kneel after catching the ball, indicating that he accepts the ball placement at the 20-yard line for the start of game play as stated in the rules. This action is called a *touchback*.

The Details of Game Play

At the start of each down, or scoring attempt, each team has the option to go into a *huddle,* the time on the field right before play begins when the two teams gather briefly on the field to discuss their next *play* prior to execution. After the huddle, they move to the *line of scrimmage,* an imaginary line which a team cannot cross until play begins.   At the line of scrimmage, the quarterback calls for the center to *snap/*hike the ball, which is passing the ball between the legs of the center to the quarterback to begin a play.

The *quarterback, or leader of the team on the field,* takes the ball and depending on the type of *play or* plan to gain yards down the field ordered by the coach, will either hand the ball off to another player, called "running" the ball, or will *pass* the ball to another player, called "passing" the ball.

The player who usually runs the ball is called the *running back* and the player who usually receives the passed or thrown ball is called the *wide receiver* or *tight end.*

Although every player position has a specified function on the field, the objective of the team is always to gain yards and score points. Therefore, while the running back, the wide receivers, and tight ends catch passes and run the ball, any eligible offensive player, including the quarterback, retains the right to run towards the *end zone, the* area each team strives to reach, with the ball to advance the team's efforts downfield to score.

Offense to Defense

The offense consists of the quarterback, running back, fullback, wide receivers, and offensive line, which includes; the center, the tight end, the left and right guards, and the left and right tackles.

11 men from each team's offensive and defensive units move to the spot on the field determined by the kickoff and the game begins. Once game play begins the offensive unit has 4 downs, or 4 scoring attempts, per possession to advance the ball at least 10 yards downfield toward the opposing team's end zone. Each time the offensive unit gains at least 10 yards on the down, the unit gains an additional four downs.

If the offense fails to gain the 10 yards needed to continue their team's advance toward the end zone within the first 3 downs (attempts), the offense may surrender the ball by *punting (kicking)* the ball back to the opposing team, the defense, with the 4th down or attempt to gain the additional yards needed to get a new 1st down. (A 4th down attempt is rare and is usually done only if the team still needs a score to win the game or if only a short amount of yardage is needed to gain the 1st down and the head coach feels confident in his team's chances for gaining the first down).

If the additional yards are not gained on the 4th down by the offense, the *opposing* team's offense takes over at the point of the last completed down.

If the offensive unit determines they have gained sufficient yards toward the end zone within the first 3 downs, but could not score a touchdown, they may decide to attempt a *field goal* kick on the 4th down that would result in 3 points if the kick is made.

> ➤ Note: If the field goal kick is missed, the opposing team would get the ball at the place on the field from which the ball was kicked.

Defense to Offense

The defense consists of the linebackers, safeties, cornerbacks, and the defensive line, which includes; the right and left defensive ends and the right and left defensive tackles. These defenders may line up in many ways to defend the field; however, there are two styles of defensive alignment which are most commonly used on teams today.

The 4-3 Defensive Front

The 4-3 defense consists of 2 defensive tackles and 2 defensive ends lined up in front of the *line of scrimmage*, and 3 linebackers strategically lined up behind them, with the cornerbacks and safeties lined up downfield.

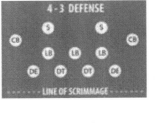

The 3-4 Defensive Front

The 3-4 defense consists of 2 defensive ends in front of the line of scrimmage, one in the middle (called the nose tackle), and 3 linebackers strategically lined up behind them, with the cornerbacks and safeties lined up downfield.

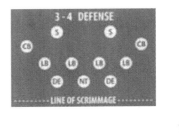

While on the field, the defense has the job of preventing the offense from gaining yards and/or scoring points during a possession. This task is performed several ways, such as:

- Attempting to *sack* the quarterback (tackling him while he has possession of the ball), which results in a loss of down and a loss of yardage as the tackle usually occurs behind the line of scrimmage.

- Applying man-to-man coverage (or man coverage), which is the use of one defensive player guarding against an offensive player's ability to catch a pass. In this coverage, the defender must stay with the receiver no matter where he runs and prevent him from catching the ball or advancing it toward the end zone. In this defensive tactic, the defender is usually focused only on a particular player.

- Applying zone coverage, which is the use of defensive players to protect and defend an area on the field. In this defense, the defender must be aware of where the quarterback may attempt to throw the ball and be ready to prevent a catch by any offensive receiver in his area of the field.

5

Scoring

How Points are Scored and Point Values

Touchdowns

The ultimate goal of the game is to score more points than the opponent, preferably by way of a touchdown. A touchdown is worth 6 points and is the highest number of points a team can earn during a single play.

A touchdown is scored player in possession of the opponent's end zone opponent's end zone.  on offense when a the ball runs with it into or catches it in the

A touchdown is scored on defense by taking the ball away from the opponent's offensive unit by *fumble, interception,* or some other defensive *turnover* and running it into the opponent's end zone.

Extra point

After scoring a touchdown, the offensive team has the opportunity to make a short kick 2 yards from the goal line through the goal post to gain 1 additional point for the team. The opponent's defensive unit remains on the field and may attempt to block the kick.

2-Point Conversion

A 2-point conversion is an opportunity for a team to score 2 additional points after a touchdown rather than the 1 normally gained by kicking for the extra point. To gain the points, the offense gets the ball on the 2-yard line and advances it across the goal line as though scoring a touchdown. In most cases, this is done only if the team attempting the points is behind or is attempting to put the scoring out of reach for the opposing team.

Field Goals

A field goal is a scoring attempt made by kicking the ball through the goalposts on the 4th down of an offensive possession when the offense is unable to score a touchdown. A successful field goal kick yields 3 points to the kicking team.

Safeties

A safety is worth 2 points and can be gained by one of the following ways: when an offensive player, quarterback, running back, or receiver is tackled with the ball in his own end zone or when a blocked punt goes out of the kicking team's end zone.

> ➤ Note: Do not confuse with the player position which is also called a safety.

Overtime

Overtime occurs when the score is tied at the end of regulation game time. To begin play in overtime, the official makes a coin toss, and just as in the beginning of the game, the team that wins the coin toss has the option to kick or receive the ball. Deferring is not an option in overtime. Currently the NFL rules state that in overtime, both teams get at least one possession of the ball, *unless* on the first possession, either team scores a touchdown or a defensive safety is made. If a touchdown or safety is scored on the first possession, the game ends and the scoring team wins. However, if neither team scores by touchdown or safety on the first possession, both team's offensive units receive the opportunity for at least one ball possession. After both teams have had the ball for at least one possession, the first team to score by any of the scoring methods, (touchdown, *field goal*, or safety), wins the game. In the regular season, if neither team scores within 15 minutes of play, (one quarter), the game ends in a tie. In the post season, play continues until one of the teams wins according to the scoring rules.

6

Officials and Penalties

Officials:

There are usually 7 officials on the field to oversee a football game:

- A **referee** who gives the signals for all fouls. The referee heads all of the officials and is the final authority on all rule interpretations.
- An **umpire** who usually rules on uniforms and equipment, as well as conduct at the line of scrimmage.
- A **linesman** who rules on all actions related to the line of scrimmage prior to or at the ball snap, such as off sides, encroachment, etc.
- A **line judge** who assists the linesman in his duties and keeps track of the time on the field.
- A **field judge** who observes the wide receivers and defenders to watch blocking techniques.
- A **side judge** who rules on plays involving receivers, including the legality of a catch, whether or not pass interference has occurred,

etc. The side judge also rules on calls involving the sidelines on his side of the field (e.g., whether a receiver or runner is out of bounds).

- A **back judge** who is positioned 25 yards down field and observes the actions of the tight ends. The back judge, along with the field judge, rules on whether field goals and conversions are successful.

Common Penalties

- **Delay of game-** A penalty called on a team for delaying the start of the game or allowing the play clock to expire before snapping the ball. This penalty results in a 5-yard loss.

- **Encroachment-** An illegal action in which a player crosses into the neutral zone, the area which is the length of the ball at the line of scrimmage, and makes contact with an opponent before the ball is snapped. This penalty results in a 5-yard loss.

- **Face mask pull-**The pulling of a player's facemask during play. This penalty results in either a 5 or 15-yard loss depending on severity.

- **False start**- Movement by an offensive player, prior to the ball snap, to indicate the start of play. This penalty results in a 5-yard loss.

- **Flag (yellow or red)**- A yellow cloth is thrown to the field by an official to indicate a foul on a play. A red cloth is thrown to the field by a team's head coach to indicate the challenge of a play.

- **Holding**-An illegal action where one player prevents another from advancing by grabbing him and holding him back. If committed by the offense, this penalty results in a 10-yard loss. If committed by the defense, it results in a 5-yard loss and automatic 1st down for the offense.

- **Intentional grounding**- Occurs when a passer, usually the quarterback, in danger of a sack, throws the ball to a part of the field where there is no eligible receiver to avoid the sack and loss of yardage. This penalty results in a 10-yard loss and a loss of a down.

- **Off sides-** Occurs when a player crosses the line of scrimmage prior to the ball snap. This penalty results in a 5-yard loss.

- **Pass interference-** Occurs when a player interferes with a receiver's ability to catch a pass by tripping him, pushing him, pulling at his arms, or any such action during play. If committed by the offense, it results in a 10-yard loss if committed by the defense, this penalty results in an automatic 1st down for the offense and ball placement at the point of penalty.

- **Roughing the passer(Personal Foul)**Flagrantly running into or hitting the quarterback after the ball has been released. This results in a 15-yard penalty and an automatic 1st down for the offense.

- **Too many men on the field-** A penalty handed out by the officials when either team has more than the allotted 11 players on the field at any time during the game. This penalty results in a 5-yard loss.

- **Unsportsmanlike Conduct-** Refers to the conduct of a player or team during a game that is deemed inappropriate, unprofessional, or in some way flagrantly against the rules of the game. This penalty results in a 15-yard loss.

➢ Note: If a penalty is incurred on a play, the head coach of the team against whom the penalty was infringed, will usually have the option to accept or decline the penalty. Depending on the option selected, the offending team may receive a loss of yardage, a loss of down, or both.

7

Fantasy, College, and Other Football Leagues

Fantasy Football

Fantasy football is not played on a field, but in homes, offices, bars, etc, by avid football fans. Because fantasy football has become increasingly popular and gains more popularity every football season, more and more fans are starting "leagues" in which to participate.

Any person can start a fantasy league as they are usually organized by average fans and are often made up of family members and friends. The participants of fantasy football are called "owners" and are a representation of team owners in a real football league. The owners organize and divide themselves into a pretend competitive football league and earn points by using the statistics of real-life professional NFL football players. *(Statistics and/or fantasy points earned are based on the number of yards gained by players from passing the ball, running the ball, receiving the ball or scoring points by touchdown, safety, field goal, or 2 point conversion).* The owners of each fantasy league *draft* or select real American football players for their teams and create a "fantasy" team using the same player positions used in a real football team. The owners are able to create their team using any combination of players from any team in the league to create their fantasy or dream team.

Depending on how well the real-life players play in their actual games in a given week, the owner of the fantasy team earns fantasy points to compete against the other owners in their created league. At the end of the season, the records of player production statistics, taken from the real football games played during the regular season, determine which teams make it to the "fantasy playoffs".

While in many ways fantasy football is organized to resemble real football leagues; fantasy football is essentially a game played amongst friends and its rules are determined by those who organize the leagues.

College Football

Like professional football, college football fans can be very passionate about this sport. As there are many colleges and universities with football programs all over the U.S., college football is arguably as popular as professional football in some areas. Many cities and towns feature college football as its primary pass time.

College football is divided into multiple divisions and conferences primarily based on the size, enrollment, and geographic area of the university. The NCAA or National Collegiate Athletic Association is the organization that oversees college athletics.

The rules that exist between college and professional football are generally congruent; however here are a few notable differences:

- There is no 2-minute warning.
- In college, a receiver catching a pass and running out of bounds, only has to have one foot inbounds for the pass to be ruled "good". In The NFL, the receiver must have both feet inbounds.
- In overtime, each team receives at least one possession of the ball at the opponent's 25-yard line and may make an attempt to score. A team may score by any of the scoring methods and the team with the highest score following its possession wins the game.

Arena Football

Arena football, unlike most other forms of football, is played exclusively indoors. It was formed in the 1980's and despite struggles in recent years, has gradually increased in popularity. Its season begins after the NFL season ends. Arena football has many fans and hosts teams in several cities throughout the U.S. As in other forms of football, Arena Football retains the basics of the sport. However there are several notable differences in this form of football.

- The game is only played on indoor football fields, usually in arenas made for basketball or hockey.
- The field of play is 50 yards long, rather than the 100 yards in NFL and college football.
- Each team has 16 men on the field of play; 8 per offense and 8 per defense.
- There is no punting due to field size.

The UFL, United Football League

The UFL is a professional football league in the United States. It was formed in 2009 and its season coincides with the NFL and college football seasons. Overall its rules are in alignment with U.S. professional and college football rules with some notable differences.

- Intentional grounding does not exist in the UFL. A quarterback may throw a ball to the ground whether there is an eligible receiver in the area or not without penalty.
- Both teams are guaranteed at least one possession in overtime.

The CFL, Canadian Football League

The CFL is the professional football league of Canada. It has a large following in Canada and has teams in several cities throughout the country. Its season runs from June through November and its championship game is called the Grey Cup. Canadian football retains the basics of U.S. football, however there are some differences.

- The goal posts are in front of the end zone. In the U.S. they are in the back.
- Canadian football is played on a field 110 yards long. In the U.S. the field is 100 yards long.
- Canadian football is played with 24 players on the field, 12 per offense and 12 per defense. U.S. football is played with 22 players on the field, 11 per offense and defense.
- Canadian football allows 3 downs to advance the ball 10 yards, while U.S. football allows 4 downs to advance the ball.

The Legends Football League

The Legends Football League (formerly the lingerie league), is an all women's American football league that was created in 2009. The game features women playing full contact football wearing uniforms consisting of shoulder pads, elbow pads, knee pads, garters, bras, and panties. There are teams in several cities throughout the United States. The Lingerie Football League retains the basics of U.S. football, with the following notable differences:

- The field of play is 50 yards long rather than the 100 yards in college and NFL football.

- The games are divided into two 17 minute halves rather than the 30-minute halves of the NFL and college football.

- There are 7 players on offense and 7 on defense rather than the 11 on offense and defense for the NFL and college.

- There is no field goal kicking or punts.

8

Football Terms

and Expressions

Game Terms

- **Audible-** A play called by the quarterback at the line of scrimmage to make a change from the play that was called in the huddle based on what he believes the defense may do.

- **Blitz-** Refers to the opposing team's defensive efforts to have multiple players attack and sack the offensive team member who has possession of the ball.

- **Check down-** A last resort short pass from the quarterback, usually thrown to a running back or tight end, when no wide receiver is open on the field.

- **Complete pass-**A thrown ball caught by the intended receiver. *(To be considered a completed pass, the receiver must have both feet inbounds and control of the ball at the time of the catch).*

- **Defensive line-** The line of linebackers and tacklers in the game to prevent the offense from advancing the ball towards the end zone.

- o **Depth Chart**-The chart showing the number of players a team has on its roster at a certain position.
- o **Down-** A down starts when the football is put into play and ends when the play is completed.

- o **End zone-**The area each team strives to reach during a scoring attempt,

- o **Extra point-** A 1-point kick, attempted after a touchdown. The kick must be kicked between the uprights and above the crossbar of the goal post (The big "H" shaped poles), behind the end zone to be considered good.

- o **Fair Catch-** Occurs when a ball is caught during a kickoff or punt and the player catching the ball on the field waves his arm indicating that he will not attempt to run the ball down field, thereby avoiding all tackling attempts by the defense. Play begins from the spot of the fair catch.

- o **Field goal-** A 3-point kick, usually performed when the team is unable to score a touchdown. This kick can be attempted from anywhere on the field, but like an extra point kick, it must be kicked above the goalpost's crossbar and between the uprights of the goalpost to earn the points.

- o **Fumble-**Occurs when a player loses possession of the football, by either dropping it or having it knocked out of his grasp, while running with it or being tackled. Under certain circumstances, a member of the team that had possession of the ball or the opposing team may recover the fumble (lost ball). If the defense recovers the fumble, it is called a turnover.

- **Hail Mary-**A last-minute throw into the end zone made by the offensive team's quarterback when his team is behind and is attempting to score points in the final seconds of the game for a win.
- **Hard Count-** Occurs when the quarterback uses the full time on the play clock, speaking loudly or "hard" as he calls for the snap of the ball. In this tactic the quarterback tries to trick the defense into believing that the ball snap has occurred in an attempt to force a defensive offsides penalty, which would reward the offense with 5 yards.
- **Huddle-**Occurs right before play begins when the members of the teams gather briefly on the field to discuss the next play for their team prior to execution.
- **Incomplete pass-** A pass that goes to the ground and is not caught by the intended receiver.
- **Interception-** Occurs when the quarterback for the team with the ball (offense) throws a ball that is caught by the opposing team (defense) rather than a member of his own team. This is also called a turnover.
- **Kickoff -** A ground kick from the tee (ball holder), made at the beginning of a game and after a team has scored to transfer possession of the ball to the opposing team
- **Line of scrimmage-**An imaginary line that a team cannot cross until play begins. The line of scrimmage is located on the spot where the ball is placed at the end of the previous down.

- **Muff-** Occurs when a player touches the ball by dropping or in some other way mishandling it in a failed attempt to gain possession. A muff usually occurs while receiving a kick or missing the ball while attempting a kick.

- **On-sides kick-** A kick made during a kickoff when the ball is kicked to the side of the field. This kick is used by the kicking team in an effort to avoid turning the ball over to the opposing team on a kickoff. Once kicked, the kicking team may not touch the ball or attempt to gain possession unless the receiving team has touched it or it has traveled at least 10 yards. The benefit of this kick is that if recovered by the kicking team, an additional possession is gained. If recovered by the receiving team, possession is gained with favorable field position; usually near the opposing team's end zone.

- **Pass protection-** An offense's blocking maneuver to prevent the defense from attacking the quarterback. Pass protection helps give the quarterback more time to pass or throw the ball.

- **Play-** A coach's offensive or defensive plan to gain yards or prevent yardage down the field during a single possession.

- **Play action pass-** Occurs when the quarterback fakes handing the ball off to the running back, and instead attempts a pass.

- **Pocket-**The area of the field where the quarterback has time to move around prior to passing the ball.

- o **Pump Fake-** A forward movement of the ball by the quarterback to fake the direction in which he will pass the ball in order to deceive the defense and gain additional time to locate an open offensive receiver.

- o **Punt-**A drop kick made on the 4th down when the offense is unable to gain sufficient yards towards the end zone to score either a touchdown or field goal. The punt kicker's objective is to place the ball as far back towards the other end of the field to cause the opposing team to have as great a distance as possible to push the ball forward towards the end zone to score points.

- o **Red Zone-** The area within the 20-yard line of the end zone.

- o **Return-**Performed when the team receiving the ball from the punt kick or kickoff catches the kick and attempts to run with it toward the end zone as far as they are able in an attempt to gain yards and ultimately score points.

- o **Running Routes-** Predetermined directional running performed by members of the offense, usually wide receivers and tight ends. The routes end in the place on the field where the quarterback will pass the ball.

- o **Sack-**Occurs when a player on the opposing team, tackles the quarterback of the offensive team behind the line of scrimmage, while he (the quarterback) still has the ball, preventing ball advancement and causing loss yardage on the play.

- **Screen Pass**-A quick pass usually thrown to the running back that features one or more offensive linemen forming a blocking "screen" against defensive tacklers which allows the runner to more easily run up field to gain yards.

- **Snap (Hike)**- The passing of the ball between the legs of the center to the quarterback to begin a play.

- **Safety**-A 2-point score the defense earns by tackling an offensive player in possession of the ball (usually the quarterback), in his own end zone. *(Do not confuse with the player position also called a safety)*

- **Secondary**- The secondary consists of 4 of the team's defensive players that play in the backfield and defend against the offensive wide receivers. (safeties and cornerbacks)

- **Shotgun Formation**-An offensive team formation on the field which features the quarterback standing several yards behind the center in preparation to receive the hike/ snap of the football to begin a play. The ball is "shot" (snapped/hiked), passed between the legs of the center to the quarterback to begin play.

- **Spiking the Ball**-Refers to a play in which the quarterback intentionally throws the ball to the ground immediately after the snap. This action costs the team one down of play and is often done at the end of the half and/or the end of the game. Spiking is a way for the team with the ball to either stop the clock to prepare for a final game winning play or to complete all downs on the possession and run the clock out, leaving no time for the opposing team.

- **Stripping the Ball-** A defensive player's method of getting the football out of the hands of an offensive player during a play, resulting in a fumble or turnover. If the ball is "stripped", but the player in possession of the ball has at least one knee down prior to losing the ball, the play is not considered to be a fumble or strip and the player with the ball retains possession.
- **Taking a knee-** Occurs when a player kneels to the ground with the ball in his hands, indicating that he will not attempt to move or advance the ball.
- **Touchback-** Occurs during a kickoff when a receiver catches the ball in his own end zone and kneels indicating he will not run the ball towards the opposing team's end zone. Play begins on the 20-yard line after a touchback.
- **Touchdown-** A 6-point score that occurs when a player in possession of the ball runs or catches it in the opposing team's end zone.

- **Turn over-** Occurs when a ball in possession by one team is lost by interception, fumble, or some other act by the defense and turned over to the other team.

- **Under center-** An offensive team formation on the field that features the quarterback standing directly behind the center in preparation to receive the snap/hike of the football to begin a play. The ball is handed (snapped/hiked) between the legs of the center to the quarterback to begin play.

Football, The Basics for Women

Other Football
Terms & Expressions

- **Chip on the shoulder-** A football and general expression that refers to a player using his own anger to fuel a better game performance.
- **Draft-** The process used to induct new players from colleges and universities around the country into the National Football League.
- **Franchise Player-** A player who might be regarded as the best player on a team and may be a player around whom a team might be built for future success.
- **Free agent-** A football player who has completed his contract with a team and is free to sign a contract with another team.
- **Icing the kicker-** An expression used when the defensive team's coach decides to call a timeout *immediately before* the ball snap for a field goal kick.

  This is done in an attempt to cause anxiety in the kicker in the hope that he will miss the kick on his next attempt.

- **Lays an Egg-**A football and general expression referring to a player or team's poor performance in a game.
- **Movin' the chains-** Refers to the chains of the orange yard measuring apparatus used by the officials to measure the number of yards gained on each down or possession of the ball.

- o **Opening Drive-** Refers to a team's first attempt in a game to move the ball downfield to try to score.
- o **Pick-** Football expression referring to an interception.
- o **Pick 6-**Football expression referring to an interception returned for a touchdown.

- o **Pigskin-**A slang term referring to a football

- o **Rookie-** A player in his first season on a professional team.
- o **Tailgating-** A pre-game party held by team fans, usually in the parking lots outside game facilities, to show support for their favorite team.

- o **Trade-** Occurs when a team exchanges one player for another player or a selection in the draft.

- o **Veteran-**A player who has played at least one complete season as professional player.

- o **2-minute drill-** Refers to a team's final scoring attempt in the final two minutes of the first half and second half of the game.

- o **12th Man-** An expression used in football referring to the perceived advantage gained by the home team due to crowd noise during the opponent's play on the field.

9

Equipment, Teams and Coaches

Cleats- Athletic shoes with grips on the bottom which allow the players to run with a lower risk of slipping.

Football- The ball used to play the game

Football Helmet-Used to protect the player's head from injury

Football Jersey- The shirt worn by players during the game that shows their name and team number.

Girdle- The supportive cup and padding worn by players to protect the area around the groin, the hips and the buttocks.

Shoulder Pads- Worn on the shoulders of the players to protect the shoulders and chest

Thigh Pads- The padding worn by players to protect the thighs.

NFL Teams

AFC North	AFC South
Baltimore Ravens	Houston Texans
Cincinnati Bengals	Indianapolis Colts
Cleveland Browns	Jacksonville Jaguars
Pittsburg Steelers	Tennessee Titans
AFC East	**AFC West**
Buffalo Bills	Denver Broncos
Miami Dolphins	Kansas City Chiefs
New England Patriots	Oakland Raiders
New York Jets	San Diego Chargers
NFC North	**NFC South**
Chicago Bears	Atlanta Falcons
Detroit Lions	Carolina Panthers
Green Bay Packers	New Orleans Saints
Minnesota Vikings	Tampa Bay Buccaneers
NFC East	**NFC West**
Dallas Cowboys	Arizona Cardinals
New York Giants	San Francisco 49ers
Philadelphia Eagles	St. Louis Rams
Washington Redskins	Seattle Seahawks

Administrative and Coaching Staff

Team Owner- The person, family, or group who owns the team.

General Manager- The person who oversees the day-to-day operations of the team. This person is responsible for making player trades, free agent acquisitions, draft selections and overseeing team salaries.

Head Coach-The top coach on staff who is responsible for team management. This person usually has the final say in game decisions.

Offensive Coordinator-The coach in charge of the offensive players. This person is responsible for the offensive game plan and usually calls the offensive plays during the game.

Defensive Coordinator-The coach in charge of the defensive players. This person is responsible for the defensive game plan and usually calls the defensive plays during the game.

Special Teams Coach-The coach in charge of the kickers. This person is responsible for developing their skills and improving their play in games.

> ➤ In addition to the primary coaches listed above, many teams have a coach in charge of each individual player position such as: quarterbacks coach, offensive/defensive line coach, receiver coach, running backs coach, linebacker coach, and secondary coach. Additionally, many teams have trainers and strength coaches who are responsible for ensuring player fitness.

Football Q & A
Answers Girls Wanna Know

**Q-Why do football players put those black
lines under their eyes?**
A-To help them see better due to the glare on the field from
lights and camera flashes

Q-Why does the quarterback lick his fingers so much?
A-To help him grip the football better during the pass.

**Q-Why does the quarterback lift his knee?
before each ball snap?**
A-To send a man, running back or receiver, to motion

Q-Why do the players slap each other on the butt so much?
A-This is usually their way of saying, "Good Job,"
or showing support to a teammate.

**Q-Why does the player running with the ball try to run
through the pile-up instead of running around it?**

A-The fastest route to a point on the field is a straight line.
Offensive players (*Offensive linemen*) are supposed to block
defensive players (*Defensive linemen*) and create spaces within
the pile so the player with the ball can maneuver through and
find a direct route down field towards the end zone.

Q-Why do the guys spit so much during the game?
A-Because they're guys

-Answers submitted by David Bowers & Angela Knapper
-53-

Made in the USA
Lexington, KY
05 October 2014